THE JOURNAL OF A
JOURNEY TO HIS HOLINESS

Bert M. Farias

Table of Contents

FOREWORD

When asked to write the foreword to this book, I was both humbled and somewhat concerned that the limited amount of time I had spent with the author in person would result in my inability to give a just and proper appraisal of this outstanding vessel of God.

God took care of that by reminding me that every time I was in brother Farias' presence the anointing draped around him like the morning dew. It reminded me of that pristine passage in Psalms 133:3 where the dew of Mt. Hermon fell on the mountains of Zion. How refreshing is the ministry of Bert Farias! I found out that you don't have to spend a lifetime to know someone. You know them by the witness of the Holy Spirit. You know them by their fruit. Therefore, I know Bert Farias.

In this must read journal, Bert has raised the bar of how your inner man can reach new horizons through submission to spiritual authority which ushers you into kingly privilege. This journal is an instruction manual on how to lay your life down, enabling the Master's will to be resurrected in you. Therefore, when you unreservedly are laid bare and open as a lamb to the slaughter, the great High Priest extracts all the rudimentary elements, thus you become a whole, burnt offering and a sweet savor to our bountiful Father. As a result, the enemy no longer has access to you as all soulish handles have been destroyed along with the wood, hay, and stubble that have no lasting value to our life or ministry. Therefore, drink deeply from the contents of this living letter and prepare to live in complete freedom and exultant joy in the Holy Ghost.

Bert Farias is a seasoned and sold out minister, far ahead of his chronological years. His messages are pregnant with purpose and content. He drinks from deep wells, moves in the Holy Spirit in the full operation of the gifts, exhibits jurisprudence in resolving conflicts, and always dips his sword of truth in honey before delivery, and above all, his signature is that he walks in humility and compassion before the Lord and his brethren.

To summarize, this gifted writer will take the reader, if they apply the truths so laid down in this journal, to the next level. Therefore, I wholeheartedly endorse, recommend, and encourage all pastors and church boards to engage Rev. Bert Farias in the future. Wisdom, truth, repentance, and an ongoing revival spirit will be your reward.

Your Covenant Bond-Servant,

Rev. Ron G. Smith D.D. Founder, Our Master's Ministries, Inc. Independence, Missouri

INTRODUCTION

In the early part of 2002 I began praying in other tongues at length. I have always made a private practice of praying in tongues quite regularly, but during this period of time I indulged in it on a daily basis. After praying for about 2 ½ months this way I then added some extended fasting for several more weeks.

Before this extended time of prayer and seeking God I had become quite frustrated with my life and ministry and a lack of certain results. At this juncture in my life I was teaching students and training young ministers on an international platform in a Stateside school of revival. I was doing everything I've always dreamed of doing. I was teaching and preaching, traveling both nationally and internationally, mentoring young students, and even found time to do some writing. My family and I were as comfortable as we'd ever been. Our finances were better than they ever were. We were in good health. We enjoyed great friendships. I had every reason to be happy and satisfied, but somehow I was not.

In my heart I was not fulfilled. There was an internal struggle. I did not have peace. I was not walking in my authority as a minister. Somehow and somewhere I was knocked out of that position of authority and it was affecting every area of my life.

Even the mentoring times with students that I so looked forward to were no longer enjoyable. After these mentoring times I would walk away emotionally and spiritually drained. I was hearing a distinct call in my spirit, "Be with Me." And so at the direction of the Lord I made a determination at the end of 2001 to put a halt to my mentoring groups, stop all extracurricular activities, limit my travels, and deepen my fellowship with the Lord.

When I first started praying in the spirit I kept having this impression of a glass ceiling over my head. On the other side of this glass ceiling was the glory, the power, the favor, the increase, and the anointing I was seeking.

While I was gazing intently at the ceiling, however, God began to deal with me about the floor, my foundation. Here are some of the first words of wisdom I heard from the Lord:

"Take away 'ministry' over the last 17 years and what do you have? Your character has not been sufficiently dealt the death blows that it will take to properly develop it to where I can impart to you the mind of Christ. You need more mortification to receive the mind of Christ."

After hearing this word is when I made the decision to add fasting to my time of seeking the Lord. After all, when combined with the Word of God, fasting is the quickest route to mortification and character transformation. And that is what this book is about.

To tell you the truth, I thought my foundation was just fine. I had been in the full time preaching ministry for about 15 years. I had been a faithful missionary. I had seen God work healings and miracles through my life. I had ministered to thousands of people in evangelistic crusades and Bible school settings and made some faithful disciples along the way. Why was the Lord directing my attention to the floor and to my foundation? The ceiling is where I wanted to go. That is what I was thinking and praying about. If I had not been in a position of humility through prayer and fasting, I would've missed it again. Thank God for His patience and long-suffering.

After several more weeks of seeking the Lord and praying, especially in other tongues, revelation began to open up to me concerning my life and ministry. It was as if the Holy Spirit was now helping me to interpret the many mysteries I had been praying out for months. For

10

several weeks I heard beautiful words. I wrote them down. God gave me a blueprint of His more perfect will for my life and ministry. In this book I've included some of the revelation I received during this time, but I've removed some of the more personal matter without excluding the truths and examples that would encourage others. Additionally, there are personal comments interjected throughout the journal.

I've written this in the first person, not to claim its infallibility, but to simply and plainly write it as I heard it. Let the Word of God judge it.

Also, the following chapters, or documents as I refer to them, are given in the order I received them. It is important to understand how the Holy Spirit builds on each piece of revelation. There is an order to it.

1 Cor 14:4 says, **"He who speaks in an unknown tongue edifies himself."** One meaning of "edify" is to organize and order. When I began to pray in other tongues at length I was organizing and ordering my life in the Spirit while edifying myself. I was accessing certain mysteries of my life and calling, and God put me on the fast track because of the time spent praying forth those mysteries. My understanding, however, was unfruitful until the interpretation of it came in these documents. Wise ministers will build their ministries this way.

There is an organization and an order in the Spirit that come as a result of the leading and direction of the Lord that you receive through prayer especially praying in other tongues. These documents are a direct result of time spent praying this way.

The apostle Paul also penned these words: **"I thank my God I speak in tongues more than you all; yet in the church..."** (1 Cor 14:18-19a)

11

As the principle writer of the New Testament, Paul's private use of speaking in tongues was his key to revelation knowledge and to his understanding of the mysteries of God. The same applies today.

This book, written in journal form, details my personal journey of how time spent praying in other tongues gave me the needed wisdom, knowledge, and understanding of God's more perfect plan for my life.

Praying in tongues is both a purifying fire and a devouring fire. As you pray in other tongues the fire of God will devour your works of wood, hay, and stubble while at the same time purifying your works of gold, silver, and precious stones. This will save your works at the judgment seat of Christ and cause you to enter into a sure reward.

How does this happen? It happens through the interpretation processes of revelation and precise instruction from the Holy Spirit. The Bible says that we should pray to interpret our heavenly language of tongues (1 Cor 14:13). The key is to locate the channel by which the Holy Spirit speaks.

Most Christians have a difficult time distinguishing their spirit from their intellect. Your conscience is the voice of your spirit. The Holy Spirit is more closely associated with your conscience than your intellect. As you pray in tongues you are praying from the channel of your conscience through which the Holy Spirit speaks.

Our problem is that we are more accustomed to looking for God's voice in our intellect. Our intellect is generally an unsafe guide because it is usually clouded with a mixture of the world's thinking where much of our decision-making is based on our best interests. Most Christians have a difficult time hearing from God because their soul which comprises of their intellect is clouded with self, mingled with the world, and yet has some Word in it.

Praying in other tongues will broaden the channel by which God speaks. In my case I prayed so much in other tongues that eventually those tongues seemed to turn to English at times, and the Lord began to give me revelation and instruction concerning my life and ministry.

Praying in tongues also aligns your heart with the motives of Jesus Christ especially as you spend time meditating on the life and words of Jesus in the gospels. This will strengthen your conscience. The conscience will then translate those motives into thoughts and order your soul in it through the revelation and instruction you are receiving from the Holy Spirit. The Spirit's purpose is to re-align your soul with the motives of Christ so He can begin to make a real bond-slave out of you. That is real character transformation which is what the Lord is after.

It is time to double up and triple up praying in other tongues, and to get the order and organization of your life and ministry from the Spirit of God. Let Him speak to you and give you clarity.

One of the main themes that has been woven into my preaching and writing over the years has been the great desire of the Spirit to save ministers and saints from dead works and laboring in vain. There are certain admonitions in scripture that have very strong application toward ministers (Mat 7:21-23) (I Cor 13:1-3) (2 Cor 3:12-15) (Jam 3:1-2). We must pay very close attention to these. To whom much is given much is required.

It is my earnest prayer that the Holy Spirit will use these documents to enlighten you, and save your works from being burned so that you will receive the Lord's reward for your labor on that day.

CHAPTER 1

WELCOME TO THE SCHOOL OF THE INNER MAN

First Instruction: After indulging for a number of weeks praying in other tongues, here is the very first piece of revelation the Lord gave me. It was here that I entered into a new grade of fellowship, and another room in the Spirit.

Welcome to My school of the inner man. Welcome to the instructions of My counsel. Welcome to the classrooms of My Holy Spirit. Welcome to the school of discipline which you were enrolled in, but have not yet graduated from. You thought the time of testing was over. You thought that only man had done this to you, but I say again that I have allowed it.

And so you are still in My school of discipline and I am requiring you to be dumb as a lamb before its slaughter. I am requiring silence from you…silence with joy…silence with kindness…silence with peace. I will not allow you to be frustrated or aggravated any more.

Personal comment: At this particular time in my life and ministry I was going through some several trials and I was constantly complaining and murmuring about things.

See that picture that's been in your spirit. See that image. You are now in between classrooms. You are leaving one room and entering into another. You are entering a new room. You are leaving the room of your youthful and unharnessed soul and you are entering into the room where your inner man shall rule. You are leaving the room of your unharnessed soul which has not had understanding and you are entering the room of greater understanding in the Spirit. You are leaving the room of the unharnessed soul and entering the room of My voice and My counsel. There will be an accuracy in hearing Me now for I am opening your ears. My counsel shall now be easier for you to receive for you have positioned yourself well.

You are moving from the classroom of man's counsel and of your own mind into the classroom of My counsel and My mind. Keep on moving. Go through that door and move on in. I have been waiting for you. I am your Counselor. I am your Instructor. I am the Ancient of Days and I know all things. I am He who taught your forefathers of faith long ago. I am ancient and yet in Me there is no time. I am He who is the wisdom for all ages and the wisdom for all times. I am beautiful for all situations. I am the joy of those who have sought me in the past and who seek Me in the present. Listen to me and do what I say and you will always succeed. I am the prosperity of all My servants. I never fail.

The work that is presently being done in you is to make you more one with Me. Then your message will mirror your inner man and fulfill every jot and tittle of your life.

You are entering a new grade of fellowship. As in school when you pass from one grade to another, even now you are moving to another grade of fellowship and instruction. I am requiring you to pass and admitting you entrance.

And you have said, "Lord, this is hard. I can't take this any more." You have looked at others and said, "Why don't you test them? They need to be tested. Those men need to be tested. They need to be purged. They need to be held back." I say to you as I said to Peter when he asked about John. What business is it of yours what I do with these other men? They are my sons and servants, too and I will do with them as I please (John 21:20-22) (2 Cor 10:12). And so you see why you have not yet passed this test? Your unharnessed soul must be subjected to My will and My counsel if you are to fulfill My high calling. Full purging is required to graduate from My school of discipline.

I know where I am leading you. And I alone know what your future holds, and I will not allow you to graduate until you have fulfilled My requirements and possess the credentials of mature sonship.

Yield to the purging process. Move on to periodical fastings even as I've put in your heart. Move on to a more complete mortification of your flesh that is executed through fasting. Move on to an increased time of the reading and meditation of My Word. Follow these promptings that are in your heart. For you are in My school of discipline and this work must be done in you. It is a work of My love. It is a work of My protection – the protection of your calling and the longevity of your oneness with Me.

It's a new day. I am taking many of My ministers who are saying yes to my high calling and taking them into My school of discipline. I am taking them into My burning furnace. I am taking them into My hot fires…the fires of purging and renewal and revival in their hearts.

It is time for My leaders and those who are called My priests to be the example that I've called them to be. It is time for the right kind of impartation to be made through them by My Spirit to the people they minister to. It is time for holiness in the hearts of every man who would bear the vessels of the Lord, who would be entrusted with the sacred work of the building up of My Church. It is time for the full consecration of all of My servants who would desire My high calling.

CHAPTER 2

PERSONAL AND MINISTRY DIRECTION

Addressing Character And Calling

Writing is a (your) key. The pen is first place. For you have always had the urge to write even in your childhood. I have put this gift in you. As you give yourself to Me in the secret place, I will open your spirit to the Word of the Lord. I will open doors for that Word to go forth into lives and into nations. You shall accomplish much by computer as My Word shall go forth from your home base.

Personal comments: It is important to organize your calling by the Spirit. Writing is a part of my calling and the Lord is putting emphasis on it here. There are some ministers who labor in certain areas that the Lord never called them to. The Bible calls this vain labor (Ps 127). No reward shall be received for this kind of labor.

Stop and think. The writings from your newsletters have always touched hearts. My Spirit has moved on those hearts who have received spiritual meat to give back to you natural monetary blessings. Your book did the same and its message will continue to be spread abroad. Others will follow. The time is now. I am opening the door. Writing is a key to opening more doors. Then you will speak and the floodgates will open, and the message will be one with the man. This is the work I do in you now...for you and your message to be one...for all of your message to be mirrored by your life.

Personal comments: Here is the work that God desires to do in every minister who is called to preach and teach the Word of God. To practice what you preach will present the greatest challenge of your life.

Hide yourself in Me, son. Keep your mouth and your tongue. I'm requiring it of you now as never before. Put your youthful speaking behind you. Put your hasty lips on hold. Bite your untimely tongue, which speaks out of turn. Speak only My wisdom. Let kindness be on your tongue. Let grace season your speech. And exchange sorrowful lips for joyful ones. Do not whine or complain, but give thanks and praise, for as you know, your words create your world (Heb 11:3).

Words, words, your negative words have created a suffocating atmosphere. You have not had sufficient breath from My Spirit. Dark clouds have been formed by your words, blocking out heaven's Son. Heaven's breeze has not blown; its sunshine has not shown because of wrong words. Gird up the loins of your mind and cease from words of strife, and you will have My life. And heaven's atmosphere shall come to you and surround you, and your peace shall be great, and your joy full, and others will partake in the shadows of this glory and on hills and on mountains I will lift their souls.

I have taught you, son. I have trained you. You have known many of these things, but your diligence in them has lacked. I have withheld certain blessings from you to protect you. I have not opened doors that you thought should have opened because of My protection. The deception would have increased in you had I opened those doors, and you would have ceased to be a man after My own heart (weeping).

I love you, My son. You're the apple of My eye. My heart takes great pleasure in the changes you've recently made and in the diligence you've begun to show. My heart takes great pleasure in the song of your voice. This is another key for you. Your singing is known in heaven. The angels partake of it. Its sounds and melodies are familiar in this place, and it is the fountain of your life.

I've put the music of heaven in your heart. The beats are My beats. The dances are My dances. Let no one despise the beats and the dances. Let no man despise the song of your voice. Let your rejoicings be in Me, and in those rejoicings you will reflect My glory.

Personal comments: "The song of your voice" was a peculiar expression the Lord coined to me. It established me in how important our ministry to the Lord is, and how much He enjoys it. Each voice is different and has its own song to sing (Rev 14:3).

My son, please know how much I love you and how much I enjoy your singing unto Me. I have created you to be with Me in the song and in the dance. This is your key to victory and to the utterances of the Lord in both your writing and your speaking.

Let us run together now, and much shall be accomplished for My will. I will return to you again and speak to you in this place. Your willingness and decision to fast for mortification and the song of your voice has positioned you to hear Me well. Continue on, My son. Continue on. I am pleased.

As they ministered to the Lord and fasted the Holy Ghost said... (Acts 13:1-3)

Personal comments: This document is a personal example of how the Lord will speak to us concerning our character and our calling. I hesitated to include it because it is personal, but decided to use it so you can learn from it and grow. There are key things here for every minister and saint.

CHAPTER 3

HASTY FEET

Take the steps I tell you to take and leave the results to Me. Don't try to figure it out in your head, but follow Me with your heart. Don't be concerned about what is *next* until you've fulfilled what is *now*. Disentangle yourself from the *next* and entangle yourself in the *now*. Remember your tendencies to run ahead. Guard against this hastiness, for I do not order the steps of hasty feet.

Hasty feet are untimely feet. They move before the time. They are out of sync with heaven's rhythm and rhyme. Slopes they come down on, but on hills and mountains they cannot climb. They are strong in the flesh, but weak in the Spirit. Do not put your trust in hasty feet. I alone will order your feet to run and not be weary as you wait on Me. And I will cause you to walk on high places and not faint.

You are in the school of discipline and part of the training is to break the bondage and yoke of hastiness off you. You must be cleared of this to fly. For they that wait upon the Lord shall mount up their wings as eagles. Wait on Me, and you will see My favor and My glory.

CHAPTER 4

MORE PERSONAL AND MINISTRY INSTRUCTION

Addressing Character And Calling

PERSONAL

Continue to seek My favor in the private place. Continue to seek My favor in the hidden places of all your heart. Do not desire the "ministry" but seek to be a blessing to the people. Be sensitive to the "little" needs of others. Seek to encourage everyone. Behold, I bring you the young man, I bring you the older man; I bring you a little child. I bring you a Nicodemus, I bring you a woman at the well; I bring you a blind Bartimeus. Give yourself to Me and I will give Myself through you for them. You will be a vessel fit for the Master's use.

Know again that many of My ministers are disapproved even as they speak. Their dual lives stop them from functioning and fulfilling My high calling. If all could be uncovered, it would be difficult for many to believe the hypocrisy which now exists. The master of deception has kept them in a place where they desire an honored reputation above the high calling. They have their reward, but only in this life.

Personal comments: The desire for an honored reputation was something the Lord emphasized during this time of seeking Him. Why is it that most ministers desire to minister in their gifts and talents above their personal relationship with the Lord? If we will be honest with ourselves, isn't it because we desire an honored

reputation above relationship?

Why do men desire to have a large organization and a large following more than they desire to build an individual life and make a disciple? Why do men seek numbers more than real fruit? The 99 more than the one? Isn't it because they desire an honored reputation above relationship with others? There's a big difference between a love for people and a lust for numbers.

Why was Timothy the only disciple Paul had who genuinely cared for the welfare of the Philippian church (Phil 2:20)? Didn't Paul have hundreds and even thousands of followers and many disciples? Why weren't any of them capable? The answer is in that scripture: Because all men seek their own and not the things which are Jesus Christ's (vs 21).

And why was the Philippian church the only church who ministered to the apostle Paul's needs (Phil 4:15)? The answer is the same. All seek their own and not the things which are Jesus Christ's.

The idol of "ministry" shall be one of the last to fall in this era of unsanctified ministry and great pride. The pride of learning and the pride of knowledge shall bow to godly wisdom, which first works in humility and in the fear of the Lord. I shall deal with the hidden insecurities and pride of many for the time has come. The full cycle of my forbearance has made its complete turn, and the cup of My zeal is full. I will deal more aggressively now with the pride of My priests until the esteem of an honored reputation shall not be desired. Much shall be exposed. Seek My favor, son, in the private place and in the hidden places of your heart for there shall be a full deliverance and great freedom your reward. Seek only My glory and obedience to My will.

The roots of your anger and impatience have been hidden underneath the soil of your desire for ministry and for an honored reputation. You've managed to hide this desire behind the ambition to disciple others. This ambition, though commendable when it is sanctified, has been diluted with a mixture of pride. Never seek an honored reputation on the earth if you desire the Lamb's fellowship. Never seek the honor of men if you desire the mind of Christ. The desire for an honored reputation among men disqualifies you from the grade (excellence) of fellowship I would have you possess with the Lamb. Seek only the honor of Him who speaks from heaven.

Wash yourself in the oil of this anointing of humility. Wash your feet in the basin of true servanthood. Take the towels of a lowly one. Cloak yourself with this holy desire until you burn only for the Master's approval, until you can say that your truest desire is to pray for the success of others.

Even though you have taught others these things, you have only possessed them in a tiny measure yourself. It is time now to step deeper into the waters of the baptism of a mature son. The transformation in you shall be great. You will love with the love of Another (my Calvary brother) and your knowledge of the Son shall greatly increase. Your understanding of His heart to please the Father shall increase. You shall take much delight in the beauty of His holiness. His great love for complete obedience to the Father shall be revealed to you and in you, and this love of obedience shall become your own.

The beauty of the **meekness** of the soul of the Son of man shall become your consuming desire. The words of the Father, "This is My beloved Son in whom I am well pleased," shall take on new meaning. And I will explode in your spirit to write.

Personal comment: As I understand it, meekness was the sum work of all God was doing in me, and this was something that was emphasized a number of times throughout this season of prayer. For this reason, you will see that throughout these documents in several

places the Holy Spirit refers to Jesus as the Lamb. The great characteristic of a lamb is its meekness.

Yes, you shall write with deeper levels of anointing now as you remain in the secret place of the Son. Yes, you shall write about the beauty of the Son and His holiness, and as you do, I will make Him desirable to My people. And by revelation of this anointing, they shall come to know the meaning of Him who is called "the Desire of all nations."

Behold the pattern Son! Behold the Beloved One! Behold what you shall become! Go and study the life of My Son. Observe Him in the gospels. Observe Him in the life of Paul who had understanding of the mystery of the Son. Let this quiet confidence which is beginning to birth in you come to blossom in the revelation of My Son. This is the anchor of your soul. This is the mind of Christ.

The time will come when you shall hear a word in your spirit like that of Ananias long ago (Acts 9). "Go and see this man. He is sick. Lay your hands on him and he shall be healed. Tell him these things." The time will come when you will hear clear and precise instructions from My counsel. In that day religious activity shall be a thing of the distant past for you shall have entered into the life of My Son. Even now My voice is clearer to you than its ever been, but as you keep on seeking Me it shall be common place for you to hear My voice and My thoughts at anytime in any place.

Continue to seek Me early and to seek Me often. Continue to make Me the first love of all your life...for all the arrangements of all your prosperity have been made, but delivery is dependent on Me remaining your first love. Put your spiritual prosperity first and every other area of your life shall prosper. For you see, it is My life in you which prospers and not your own. You've had My blessings, but you've tasted little of My prosperity.

The hearing of My voice and the leading of My Spirit is My prosperity. Knowing My mind is My prosperity. Take it. Possess it. Receive it. Be transformed into My image and it shall be said of you as those of old: "Behold, the peace and the prosperity of Your servant is great." But know this, that the prosperity of a son is to be much greater than that of a servant. Enter in, My son, for the table has been prepared. Enjoy the prosperity of your sonship. Receive My grace. Receive My peace multiplied.

MINISTRY

Now I will speak to you concerning ministry. In order for the streams of the anointing that are in you to more frequently emerge, there must be a thorough work done on your insides. For you have known that there is an inside-ness about your call, and it has been hidden because you have operated more from the outside in. The unharnessed soul and the unruly activity of soulish desires, which hinders fruit bearing, have stood in the way of the sanctified and more perfect ministry. Your recent hunger has opened the doors again to My school of the inner man where you will learn to subject your soul to the disciplines of My Spirit.

You will minister now with more brokenness. You will minister in weeping. You will minister in joy and in more revelation and power. You will now minister more from the inside out, and your boldness shall be tempered with the meekness and humility of the Son. And you will acquire deeper levels of purging as you obey Me in the disciplines (thereby purging out the old leaven of soul ties).

Personal comments: The disciplines the Lord spoke to me about were private worship, praying in other tongues, fasting, and meditation and confession of the Word of God.

Your prayer activity shall now become a life of prayer. Your lack of diligence in fasting shall now become a life of fasting. As you know,

My love for you is the same whether or not you pray and fast, but My perfect mind for you will not be made manifest without it. My perfect will, plan, and purpose for you will not be made manifest without it. You see, it's up to you son, but now because of your recent willingness to humble yourself, I give you more grace.

Personal comments: The more true humility you demonstrate the more grace the Lord releases; and before honor is humility.

You are moving away from the law and further into the glorious liberty of the Son of man where He Himself said in the volume of the book, "I delight to do thy will, oh God." In your obedience to the discipline of My Spirit shall spring forth a fullness of delight which you've not yet known as a permanent place in your soul. This delight shall emerge as the unbridled activity of your unharnessed soul shall submerge. And the desire of the Son in you shall turn your soul toward the Father. The fleshly soul shall be burned and the spiritual soul shall be turned toward the Father. His ways and His will shall be engraved on your soul. And His works shall be manifest through your life.

Your thinking has already been greatly elevated from the place you were in just three months ago. Your conversation has also now in it the tones of a purer love. This is already the firstfruits of a greater awareness of My Spirit. It is a manifestation of John 7:18. Today you have become more one with My Word, and the ears of your spirit have been more keenly awakened. But be on constant watch and beware of the deception of the heart to align itself with the subtleties that are a part of the unharnessed soul.

Personal comments: "He who speaks of himself seeks his own glory..." (John 7:18). A greater awareness of the Holy Spirit reduces self-seeking, and produces a stronger love walk. The Lord kept speaking to me about how the desire for an honored reputation keeps many from a deeper fellowship and identification with the

Lamb.

Beware of the smoothness of the thoughts of the unharnessed soul. Beware of its subtle and proud human reasonings which disguise itself as humility and wisdom. It will be difficult for you to detect these reasonings except you remain in Me.

CHAPTER 5

TRUE AUTHORITY

GIVING

Look not to the ideas and strategies of other men. Do not imitate the ministries of man for I Myself will give you counsel and at times unconventional instructions. Relationships shall be strengthened through such means and the example of it shall bear much fruit. Your giving shall strengthen your relationships. Always look to sow and not to reap for it is more blessed to give than to receive.

Personal comments: This is the true meaning of "a man's gift making room for him."

But in the end you will always receive more than you give because I am your God, and My laws of giving and receiving are established.

As you do these simple things and seek to always give, the word "ministry" shall take on new meaning for many have abused their authority. Look to Me and not man for all your wisdom and counsel. Listen to Me as men speak. The instructions I give you shall not always make sense to your natural mind. Allow Me to be your total Source for all things.

PRAYING

Opportunities, finances, and promotion is not the end goal and primary purpose of your ministry. It is the people. I love people. Pray for the people as if they were all your children, and then you will have My great heart for them. Then you will have the heart of a true intercessor. Oh, how lacking are true hearts in ministry today! How so many of My people have been prostituted by the greed and covetousness of ministers who speak with great swelling words of flattery!

Oh My son, do not identify yourself with these things. Do not partake of their evil deeds. Put on bowels of mercy. Bear in your heart My affections for My people. Clothe yourself with the garments of the true priesthood who stand in the gap for those in need, who would rather suffer than see others suffer, and who willingly suffer on their behalf, who love unconditionally even when mistreated, and who never revile. As you continue to wait on Me, the work of meekness as in Isaiah 42:1-3 shall be branded on your soul, and to many it shall be an enigma.

Personal comments: One of the meanings of meekness is the ability to not react in the flesh to a situation; to keep your emotions under the influence of the Holy Spirit. This ability marked the life and ministry of Jesus. An enigma would mean that you would be so transformed into another person that those who formerly knew you would not recognize you as the same person.

MATURITY IN LOVE

I am going to give you insight now into the ministry of the pastor for you have inquired. The reason I give no example in the New Testament of a single pastor led church is because the honor of such a ministry belongs to the Lamb who was slain and purchased sole possession of the sheep through His precious blood. If more of My shepherds would esteem the holy blood, they would never again exercise control over My sheep nor abuse their authority. Instead they would only desire to also lay their lives down for My sheep. Wherever this selfless compassion is found among My shepherds, you will find true authority.

But I would remind you and have you know that I honor all authority even that which is controlling and abusive. That is why I told My disciples to obey the law from those who sat in Moses' seat. That is why Paul apologized for his dishonorable behavior and language before the high priest. But I call My sheep to follow Me. I know them and they know Me. They submit to Me based on relationship and not requirement. They submit to Me based on their knowledge of Me. That is the example I have left in scripture for you to follow.

Personal comments: Therefore, a lack of submission to authority is due to a lack of respect and knowledge of the Word of God.

Many get entangled in the technicalities of authority issues and miss the Spirit. Spirit is before structure and relationship is before requirement. That is My best. Nevertheless, I will honor all authority for that is My Word. I will deal with men's pride and insecurities as they yield to Me and give Me place in their lives and ministries. The time of Mat 7:21-23 is at hand where the motives of men's hearts shall be pressed by the Word of the Lord. This will be revolutionary for many due to the soul ties they have with their programs and their structures. And the love of money and earthly securities has many bound to the system of unbelief. Yet I will deliver many whose cry is for truth and freedom. And I will put My love for My sheep in My shepherds, and they shall feed My sheep as I feed them.

There is no law in the New Covenant but only the law of My Spirit who is present and moves to lead and guide where there is My love. There is law and there is love. I would have you stay in love.

Maturity in love is required for the unity and flowing together of My leaders. Maturity in love is required for the correct use of authority. Maturity in love is required for the submitting of My leaders and My people one to another.

It is My love people submit to. It is My love in you that people are drawn to. Any measure or motive or method that is outside of My love is a cheap substitute for true authority. Many of My people have become prostitutes to substitutes, but there are some who want it that way. For some that is easier than real love that speaks the truth. Some of My people fear the truth because they've not been developed in love. Just as pride and insecurities in My leaders have caused them to move in a counterfeit authority not according to truth and love, even so the pride and insecurities in My people have caused some to run away from truth and love and submission.

I anoint truth in love. I cannot build on the lies and falsehood of the vain traditions and doctrines of men, but where there is love, I forbear with a certain measure of ignorance and tradition. But I will gradually detach Myself from places where truth is spoken with no love. All of My authority is an authority based on love and relationship. Seek to serve others for that is My love in manifestation and true kingdom authority.

PRIESTLY MINISTRY EQUALS KINGLY PRIVILEGE

There is springing up a word in your spirit concerning "hiding." I would have you hide yourself in Me without hiding yourself from the fellowship of man. Although you are in a season of separation from man, separation does not mean isolation. Higher fellowship does not mean isolation from lower forms of fellowship. I would have you be on alert and on guard against carnal forms of fellowship, but to be a blessing by carrying My presence and distributing My love among the brethren. I will teach you to de-elevate your thinking to fellowship with man in a non-reactionary way and where your spirit is not suppressed.

Having said all of that, I will now speak to you of the hiding. It is a place in the Spirit that even among the crowds you will have fellowship with Me, and hear My wisdom and My counsel and move in My love. You must determine to stay in this place whether alone or in a crowd or with a group of people. When you are grieved or you sense Me calling you away, then you must do so.

I will now choose your friends. I will reconnect you with some old and connect you with some new.

Personal comments: Solomon was a wise householder. In 2 Chronicles 5 he assembled the old proven ministers (elders, heads of tribes, chief elders) with the new (Levites, priests, their sons and brethren) in order to restore a fresh anointing which ushered in the glory cloud of the Lord.

I am teaching you to be more selective about who you open your heart to without being suspicious of anyone. In My love there is discernment but not suspicion. This is where you have fallen short in the past. You mistook discernment for suspicion because you were not operating in the Spirit or My authority. Actually, you only recently have been restored to the authority you've been out of for years. But now because of My grace I not only restore the lost authority, but I am adding to it (a true mark of restoration).

But know this: your high calling is to Myself and long seasons of solitude. Your highest calling that will yield maximum fruitfulness and true kingdom increase is in your "hiding" and your solitude. I will supply the wisdom and the helpers you will need for administration (or any other need that arises).

You are moving from youthful ministry to that of a mature son. Your stature has now changed. A new authority is emerging in you. I give you the counsel for righteous leadership. Do not be unequally yoked with the unrighteous (acts or individuals who would persuade you or influence you away from your yieldedness to the Lord). Do not be unequally yoked with youthfulness. I speak to you now as one with rank. I now give you ambassadorial stature for My Word shall go out from you to the nations. You are now to speak, dress, and conduct yourself in an ambassadorial manner. Leave what you were behind. Put away old images out of your mind. Step over the threshold and into this new anointing and into the image of My Son.

Study the stature and demeanor of the ambassador. Study and behold the ambassadorial stature of the Son. I stamp this image in you. Possess it. Receive it. It is for My honor and my honor alone.

Do not be jealous for the administrative busyness, responsibility, and positional authority of others. Your authority shall not come from these things. You are a priest and your authority is priestly. Your garments are praise. Your sacrifice is fasting and intercession. Tears are your joy when you know and I allow you to see what their manifestation births. As your private priestly ministry and authority grows I will grant you kingly favor and royal privilege. You will walk on red carpets and fly first class. Remember, kingly privilege comes from private priestly ministry.

You will walk on high places of kingly privilege and also feast with those of priestly rank.

CHAPTER 6

WISDOM FOR ADMINISTRATION

Now let Me give you wisdom for administration. Let the fruit grow the ministry, and not the ministry grow the fruit. Don't try to make room for your gift, but let your gift make room for you. For you, administration is to follow ministration. Do what I tell you and don't add to it.

Behold the Son as He fed the multitudes! Behold the simplicity of His administrative instructions to the disciples. He did not tell them to gather the remains until everyone had eaten and were filled. He did not think of gathering and preserving the fruit until there was fruit. There was a certain administration that followed the ministration. The Son did not say, "Let's see what we can get back from this miracle." Freely He received and freely He gave. Have the same mind-set as that of the Son. Be liberal in the distribution of all your ministration. I will tell you when, and teach you how to negotiate when it is a time for negotiation.

I hear you saying, "Make it plain, Lord. Break this instruction down for me into more practical terms. Give me examples of this." I will do that for you. For example, in _____, I opened the door there. The ministration brought forth fruit. The translation of the book is something I led them also to do. Now you negotiate.

But at one time, if you'll remember, you were trying to take advantage of the momentum there and you spoke of planning a big crusade and bringing some interns down to help, etc. What you were doing was planning to add to the ministration. You were attempting to add to what I was doing. Actually, you do this more often than you would like to admit. You do it at the school here. You do it with your classes. You do it with your ministry trips. It is habit (a soulish habit) that must be broken now by My counsel.

Also, as another example of the ministry growing the fruit, I give you the_____. If you will be honest with yourself, in your mind you are already attempting to have conferences and crusades there. It's right and it's godly to follow your relationships. It's right and it's godly to share vision, but be careful, My son, not to think of ministry first.

Behold the ministration of the Son again as He fed the multitudes. He was not thinking ministry. He was not thinking of opportunities for self-promotion. He was not thinking of ways to utilize the momentum of the ministration. The Son did quite the opposite of that. He often withdrew from the multitudes and never did He need to create ministry for fruit. That is only for those who lack the power and the true ministry of My Spirit. Opportunities are limitless to the man who walks in My revelation and power.

Personal comments: Opportunities are also limitless to the man who knows when God's perfect timing says, "Draw out now" and miracle wine fills human clay pots with God's Spirit.

The Son was not thinking ministry when He fed the multitudes. He loved the people. He had compassion on the people. The compassion of His heart brought forth the fruit of needs being met. Your ministry will also grow from the fruit of your compassion. Again I say, let the fruit grow the ministry and not the ministry grow the fruit. This is a common error in ministry today, and it is a testimony again, of the powerlessness and the lack of true authority in My leaders. True authority is born from compassion.

Personal comments: This paragraph absolutely revolutionized my life and ministry. It stopped me from pushing in the flesh for certain

results and produced a rest in my soul.

It is fine to send out tapes. It is fine to publish books. Print brochures and put out videos as I lead you. Let people know what you are doing, but let all these things be born of compassion. Let compassion birth forth the fruit I ordain, and let the fruit grow the ministry to the scope I also ordain. Let all your planning be rooted in Me and in My compassion.

Behold the counsel of My Spirit producing compassion, might, and true authority in you! Continue to seek My counsel which is plentiful and sufficient for all your needs. I know everything. Keep on coming (and yielding) and I will keep on counseling. I love you and have many plans for you to prosper and bring you an expected end.

Avoid the temptation to always want to know more than I am willing to disclose to you at any set time and season. Remember that your entire walk is a walk of faith, one step at a time. You cannot bear all that I want you to eventually know with time. Your human nature could not handle it. But as you prove your faithfulness in the little I will give you more. Right now I am giving you My counsel in a measure. I am reminding you of things you know and admonishing you in them so that you may do them, for there has been a deception from hearing and not allowing these things to work in your heart until you are doing them.

I am building on the counsel I've already given you. I am saying certain things in a different way and from a different angle so that you will understand it and grasp it. Do not seek more counsel as much as you seek the Counselor. And do not lose heart or lose confidence when new counsel is not given. The counsel I've already given you is sufficient for the present needs and contain much grace to catapult you into a fruitful future.

As you continue to walk with Me and seek Me and learn My voice and prove faithful to the measure of counsel I now give, I will give you another measure. There will come an even higher caliber of counsel with more details and specific instructions. You should not be anxious for that day because more will be required of you. With every measure of My counsel comes responsibility and greater warfare to those who disobey.

Be content, My son with the wisdom of your Father for you. Be content and trust in His order of the times and seasons for you. Don't be concerned about what you don't know, but be responsible for what you know. Responsible sonship breeds authority in fatherhood. Your effectiveness in fathering shall be in proportion to your responsibility to My counsel.

Seek not higher counsel for with it comes higher warfare. Leave it to Me as to what, when, and how much counsel and instruction and direction I give you. Be content in My fellowship and in the manner in which it manifests.

CHAPTER 7

THE MANAGEMENT OF HOME (DOMESTIC) AFFAIRS

Personal comment: I heard the phrase 'domestic affairs' and knew the Lord wanted to talk to me about my home life.

You have done well, but I would have you make minor home improvements. You have done well to let your wife guide the house and be the queen of domestic affairs.

One adjustment you can make is to not separate what you call ministry time, studying and praying, from the natural work that needs to be done in and around your home. For I will be with you in those menial tasks; I will speak to you and give you revelation, and there will be a freshness and a peace and a grace even during those times. Be with Me even in those menial tasks for My Spirit is with you always. The Spirit desires to teach you and counsel you even during those times. So praise Me and give thanks for My participation and co-laboring with you in those domestic affairs.

Put on the cloak of servanthood in your home chores, in running errands, and doing the menial tasks. Be clothed with humility and in that spirit of humility and servanthood I will continue to visit you and refresh and renew you in My love, and I will teach you concerning My ways.

You are also to sing while you work for it is in your light-heartedness and in your praise and rejoicing that you will continue to reflect My glory.

Personal comments: This is the second or third time the Lord has spoken to me about singing and praising Him. It is obviously something He wants me to cultivate. By nature I am not a real cheerful person but have tendencies to be serious, intense, and even melancholy. Making melody in your heart keeps your spirit light as a feather.

I desire oneness with you in both the spiritual and the natural affairs of life for in My kingdom there is no separation (this is a great truth). Let My kingdom come to that part of your life which you call natural. And let the King of glory and the Prince of peace rule in your heart during those times.

Do not separate your time spent with your wife and your son from your time spent with Me. Spend time with your family with Me. I say it to you another way: Enjoy Me with your family. This is another reason for your impatience and frustration. This stems from the residue of religion and performance that is still left in you. Even this morning in your time with your wife you were allowing some impatience to brew in you because of your desire to run to the woods and commune with Me there. I am not in the woods. I am in your heart. I am with you in the woods, but I am also with you when you are with your wife and son.

You are not rightly dividing in your heart the reality that I am always and everywhere with you. This is a lack in you being aware of My presence. This is religion all over again. You must learn to relax when you are not in solitude with Me. There is a time to be alone with Me. There is a time to be with your family. There is a time to be with other people. Enjoy Me in every setting. Be aware of My presence with you in every setting.

Your frustration and impatience stems from not hearing My daily assignments for you. Often you are tossed between having time in prayer, and the Word, or just doing administrative tasks, or being with your family in a relaxed way. Doing what I assign should free you from the burdens of the flesh. Listen to Me. I will give you assignments and order your day. Frustration will cease, your time will increase, and you shall walk in My way.

CHAPTER 8

THE MEAT OF OBEDIENCE

It is required of My servant-sons that they be obedient above all else. The desire for obedience must be the delight of all who would follow the **Lamb.** This is the mind of Christ. The desire for obedience is preferred above the desire to hear My voice and receive My counsel. For what profit is there in hearing My counsel and not obeying it?

The meat of obedience was the **Lamb's** food. The meat of obedience was the core value of His entire life. Even when He was seen in the temple at 12 years of age, he was surprised to find that His parents did not know that He was about His Father's business. The great delight of the **Lamb** was to do the Father's will. He had no desire to initiate any action or assignment outside of the will of His Father. The **Lamb's** love for the Father manifested even to the obedience of the death of the cross.

Behold the **Lamb** in Gethsemane! Behold Him in the garden of His greatest trial as He sweat great drops of blood! Behold Him at the scourging post! Behold His desire to drink the cup when His flesh and natural man cried out against it! With the horrors of His separation from the Father facing Him, behold how He prayed that the Father's will would be done!

I search the hearts of men for this perfect heart. I search the hearts of men and test them with small acts of obedience. I search the hearts of men to see if they are willing to do what I say. I will not say what I know they will not do. Where there is not this willing heart of obedience there is not love strong enough to receive even a portion of the mind of Christ.

Where is the love of the **Lamb** among My people? Why should I give My counsel to the disobedient? In my mercy I have chosen not to give many My counsel lest their insufficient character brings an accusation against them and causes a curse to come. Many have not even developed sufficient character to even obey My written counsel. So why should I reveal My hidden counsel to those who are not even obedient to My written (revealed) counsel?

I would have you understand the depths of the meaning of the words of My Son, "I delight to do thy will, oh God; yes, Thy law is within My heart." This is the work I desire to do in those who are willing to follow the **Lamb.** When this purging work is done so that this more perfect heart is developed in them then I will grant them a greater and greater capacity to hear instructions fit for mature sons. I will open their ears.

My love must mature in My children so that they will obey Me. He who loves Me keeps My commandments. Then will I manifest my glory in him and My Father and I will make our home in him and share our counsel.

My commandments are not grievous because they come with grace and truth. Grievous commandments would be those meant for the mature that are given to the immature. I am a good Father and I do not put a yoke on any of My children that will gender bondage. Satan is the one who will use the flesh and the carnal mind of man to put requirements on My children that I have not even placed on them Myself (this is why discernment is the measuring rod of maturity).

Personal comments: The meat of obedience was the core value of the Lamb's life (John 4:34) (2 Cor 10:3-5). Notice how many times the Holy Spirit refers to Jesus as the Lamb. He brought this to my

attention after I had read this document multiple times. It is an image that He wanted to engrave on my soul that would lead to greater transformation. This delight to do the will of the Father comes through the fear of the Lord and meekness of soul which were qualities of the Lamb of God.

CHAPTER 9

LEARNING TO HEAR

All this time I've been giving you certain instructions to see if you would be willing to do it. As you obey Me in these less bizarre and easy to receive instructions, I will eventually give you more bizarre instructions that make less sense to the natural mind. This is why your mind must be developed to think more like My mind, and your heart must also be developed to trust Me when I speak.

Your willingness and delight in doing My will is only a part of the equation. For you, I already know that if you knew without a doubt that it was Me speaking to you, you would obey Me instantly. Where you need development is in your confidence. That is why I'm giving you easier instructions now so you can see the fruit of your obedience and then you can have a confidence that you are hearing Me. This is how I will develop both your mind to think like Me and your heart to trust in Me.

I desire to develop you to such a place of hearing My voice that it becomes second nature to you. I desire to develop your mind and your heart to a place where you can hear My voice anytime and anywhere. I desire to develop your ability to hear Me immediately without delay and in the most minor details of life. I desire to make you skillful and accurate in hearing Me where you will never have to feel like you're guessing or assuming.

To hear Me and obey Me is the secret to all of My power. All things shall then be made possible unto you.

Personal comments: At this juncture the Lord spoke to me to sow a

fairly large financial offering into another ministry. When I first heard this instruction I was not fully willing to do it and even doubted it was from the Lord. He used it to further teach me on hearing His voice. He showed me how many of His people talk themselves out of obedience. Obedience without question is the place the Lord wants us to come to.

Obedience in these kind of instructions are things that I will use in developing your trust in hearing and obeying My voice. And as you do, I will enlarge your capacity to hear and your trust in obeying Me.

These shall be great lessons in faith. You have learned faith in the classrooms of man, but now you will learn faith in My classroom. For I would have you step higher into the real life of faith. I would have you step higher into the simplicity of this life. The simplicity of it comes from hearing Me and obeying Me, and then leaving the results to Me. You are not responsible for the fulfillment of the Word you hear and obey. You are only responsible for obeying what you hear. But as your confidence and trust to hear Me and obey Me is developed, your faith shall also be developed as you watch Me perform My Word. In that day life shall be so different for you.

I will take you from one level of hearing and obeying My instructions for yourself to another level of hearing and obeying for ministry to others. Your faith shall grow by leaps and bounds because of your ability to hear being developed. How shall you work the works of God unless you hear the words of God? How shall you co-labor with the Counselor in My works if you do not hear his words? Hearing and obeying, words and works…This is the real life of faith and of My Son.

This is the living Word I spoke to you about which produces hearing first and then the action. This is the real faith. And so know that the living Word is finding a greater place of lodging in you. It is the hearing of My Word in your spirit that makes it a living word. It is the hearing of it in your spirit that produces the life and the actions of My Son.

CHAPTER 10

SONGS

SONG OF HIS OBEDIENCE
My Meat and My Delight

My delight is obeying the Father
My delight is in walking as the Son
My delight is in following the Spirit
My delight is in walking as one

To run my race with patience
To finish my course with joy
To preach the gospel of this grace
That is my meat and my delight

My meat is obeying the Father
My meat is in walking as the Son
My meat is in following the Spirit
My meat is in walking as one

SONG OF HIS COUNSEL
Dilemmas

There's no more dilemmas in life
For I have been given His counsel
All of my problems now to resolve
By His immutable counsel

The ear of my spirit He has opened
And there's no more dilemmas in this life
There will be no more failures
And no more groping in the dark

For He has lightened my way with His counsel
And He has paved my way with the sword of His love

The path of the just shines brightly
With each new passing day
The path of the just shines so brightly
By the light of His counsel that He's put in my way

My soul has become as a watered garden
My spirit refreshed by His Word
There's no more confusion and strife in my mind
For the light of His counsel is now mine

He leads me beside the still waters
He makes me lie down in green pastures
He anoints my head with oil
He restores my own soul

The Lord is my shepherd forever
I shall never ever want
The Lord is my shepherd forever
I am His sheep and I shall never want

There is no lack in my life
For the light of His counsel has been given to me
Never have I seen the righteous forsaken
Nor his seed begging for bread

Though the young lions lack and suffer hunger
They that seek the Lord shall never lack for any good thing

This is the grace of my Father
This is the love of my Christ
This is the communion of the Holy Ghost
And I am so blessed by all

This is the grace of my Father
This is the love of my Christ
This is the communion of the Holy Ghost
And my life of dilemmas is all but gone

SONG OF HIS PLANTING
Like a Tree

Blessed is the man who seeks the Lord
Blessed is he who walks not in the counsel of the ungodly
Blessed is he who stands not in the way of sinners
Blessed is he who sits not in the seat of the scornful
Blessed is he whose delight is in the law of the Lord

Blessed is the man who seeks the Lord
For he shall be like a tree planted by the rivers of water
He brings forth his fruit in its season
His leaf also shall not wither
And whatever he does shall prosper

Oh, I am that tree
For I have partaken of His counsel
And I would like to say
That I am that tree

I'm a tree planted by the Father
And no man can pluck me from the palm of His hand

I'm being planted, I'm being planted
By the light of His counsel
I'm being planted, I'm being planted
By the strength of His Word

I'm being planted, I'm being planted
By the rivers of water
I'm being planted, I'm being planted
I am that tree whose fruit shall never fail

Personal comments: I spoke and sang these psalms in to a mini recorder and then transcribed them in to this document. They teach and admonish us that obedience to the Spirit's counsel results in His planting. Each psalm emphasizes one of these components.

CHAPTER 11

RELIGION

Think back to your former days when in your innocence and simplicity you possessed a certain awareness of the reality of My presence. Surprisingly, as your knowledge of My Word increased, you forfeited a portion of that awareness. "Ministry" spoiled the innocence and simplicity of our fellowship. Your mind became somewhat corrupted by "ministry." Religion entered back into your life in a different form and worked a measure of death birthed by the works of man.

If you will be honest with yourself and remember those former days, you will have to admit that you had an awareness of My presence not only in your solitude with Me, but on the job as well. You had a sensitivity to the sinner and were always aware of Me when in their presence. But then after being trained for ministry, and being always around believers, performance and activity became the king of all your service. A measure of My love was diminished and a measure of My awareness was lost. Religion again worked its course in you to separate you from Myself.

Put away all residue of religion and move on into the glorious life and liberty of the Son. Move on into the communion of the Holy Spirit in all phases of your life.

I would have you know that My Son was the most un-religious person that ever walked the face of the earth. He was the last Adam. What the first Adam possessed before the fall, the last Adam possessed without ever falling. In the first Adam, before the fall, there was no religion. There were no temples made with human hands. There were no religious groups and denominations. There was not to be in the original purpose of the Godhead a division among men concerning religious persuasion or doctrine. These things are now all a product of sin and of the curse that came upon the earth.

There was no division between the spiritual and the natural. My kingdom was a part of all of Adam's life. There was no division between his ministry to Me and his personal life. It was all one.

As I have already spoken to you, one of the greatest idols in these last days that will bow its knee to My presence is the idol of "ministry". "Ministry" has a subtle way of spoiling the simplicity of a walk with Me. The idol of ministry is birthed by the spirit of religion. It is man using My Word to do their own will in ministry. That is the reason for so much of the division that exists in My body today.

In My Holy Spirit of Truth there is no division. If all men would learn to humble themselves and bow their wills to My life and My mind, the Spirit of Truth would teach them. My true life and liberty has been sacrificed on the altar of the stubborn will of man. The Spirit of Truth has been quenched by the muddy waters of religion that works through the will of man.

I would have you know, son, that it was the filthy hands of religion that crucified the innocent clean hands of My life on that cross. It is still the filthy hands of religion today that crucify My life on the altar of the human will of man. It was the filthy hands of the religious spirit that opposed and then crucified the glorious life and liberty of the Son. Lucifer so opposes this life and liberty that is found in My Son because it defies religion and the selfish will of man.

Study Isaiah chapter 14. See how Lucifer fell. Hear what he said.

Was it not his will that opposed Me and My reign? Lucifer's will desired exaltation. A desire for an honored reputation led to his fall. He has great hatred for all mankind, but especially toward those who only desire to do the will of the Father, and not their own.

That is why the Son uttered phrases like, "I came not to do My will, but the will of Him who sent Me." "…My judgment is just because I seek not My own will, but the will of the Father which has sent Me." "And My delight is to do Your will, oh God." Statements like this were like a slap to Lucifer's face.

In the depths of that delight to do the Father's will lies the secret of deliverance from the spirit of religion. It is all found in the will. The key is to surrender your will on the altar of His life.

In the hearing and obeying of My counsel lies the secret to possessing that life. That life is a life of liberty that is free of religion. Religion is based on activity and performance outside of hearing and obeying. Liberty comes when you hear and obey what I say. Doing your own will genders bondage.

The only kind of religion that is pure is the kind written in James 1:27 which is to take care of widows and orphans and to keep oneself unspotted from the world.

This is a living word which produces a living faith.

CHAPTER 12

PURE RELIGION

James 1:27---My captains are found among these just as the Son was found among them. I do a work in you of pure religion. I do a work in you to place you among My captains. I do a work of love in you. I do a work of sensitivity to My heart in you.

Behold My heart as I was moved with compassion for the widow at Nain whose son had just died. Behold My heart as I picked up the little children and blessed them. Behold My heart as I called and healed the blind beggars.

I do a work in you to increase the fruit of your compassion. I do a work in you to increase true ministry. I do a work in you to make you more skillful in My anointing. As you've heard My servant say, "Truth and compassion equal skill in My anointing." I speak the truth, but I am moved with compassion.

Truth does not move Me. Compassion moves Me. I am working both on your speaking and on your compassion so that your life and your works would be found pure in Him who moves.

This is the alignment of My Spirit to continue to build those mysteries in you of which you've prayed. This is the alignment of My Spirit to build into you true priestly ministry. This is My armor for you.

I am tightening your belt of truth. I am firming you up with the breastplate of My righteousness. I am strengthening your arms to hold up the shield of faith. I am shodding your feet with a greater preparation of the gospel of peace. I am protecting your mind by having you renew it with My salvation. I am sharpening your sword of the Spirit.

You are asking Me about pure religion. "What is it that makes visiting the fatherless and the widows in their affliction pure and undefiled?" I hear you asking.

I will answer you in segments. First of all, you have had a recent prompting in your spirit concerning this book (James). There is a reason for this. You see many of the mysteries you have recently prayed have come from this book.

Personal comments: I was spending much time praying in other tongues and this was a real revelation to me. Apparently it is possible to be praying mysteries in the Spirit concerning an entire book, epistle, or chapter in the Bible especially as it pertains to your own life.

The work I do in you is found in much of this book. It is a work of removing the impurities and the obstructions from your life so that your works will be found pure in the day of the testing of my fire.

I am requiring a living faith from My people in this hour. How much more My priests and My captains? You have been weighed in the balance and been found lacking in genuine faith. This is why I speak to you of pure religion.

I am giving you wisdom for your trials. Trials remove the impurities. Trials produce a patience of character where you become mature and complete and lacking in nothing. This is the work I do in you. These are the mysteries you've been praying before Me. Now I give you more understanding.

I am speaking to your character. I am speaking to your calling. In both your character and your calling I am commanding the image of the Son to arise in you. Your prayers have not been in vain. I have come to reveal the mystery of Christ in you, the hope of glory.

The Son was pure before and after He entered public ministry. With and without the anointing He was pure. His private words and works matched His public words and works. James knew this well.

Personal comment: The reason for this is that James was the natural brother of Jesus and lived in the same house.

This is My perfect will for all My children especially those who are ministers of My Word in public service. My perfect will is for all religion to be pure.

For religion to be pure, all impurities must be gone. All hypocrisy must be gone. All partiality must be gone. Acts of mercy and good fruits must not be found wanting.

The leaven of the Pharisees was hypocrisy. They said many things but did not do them. Their hearing and their speaking did not culminate in good deeds. They judged the shortcomings of others while overlooking their own.

Hypocrisy also manifests in a double tongue. A man's religion is vain and useless when he cannot bridle his tongue, when blessing and cursing proceed out of the same mouth, when praise and then murmuring and complaining comes gushing forth. Remember, it is what comes out of a man's mouth that defiles him.

Such is the case in many of those who call themselves by My name. That is why I have told you that the work I do in you is to make you one with your message. Your words must be mirrored by your works, and your words must be found pure at all times. You have been walking in that which has been permissible, but now I am calling for the perfect to come.

Partiality is another impurity that defiles My people. Partiality is being a respecter of persons. It respects the rich while despising the poor. It receives the rich for what they can give, but despises the poor because their needs require acts of sacrifice and compassion. Partiality honors what it can get, but dishonors what it can give. The needy suffer because of the partiality of My people. My mercy is shut up in the bowels of My people. Many of them are unfamiliar with the Father of mercies.

God is the Father of pure religion. You will find His pure works birthed among the poor and needy. You will find the bondservants of His Son in the avenues of the despised, in the streets of the oppressed, and in the homes of the broken and downtrodden.

Pure religion is that which is without hypocrisy and partiality, full of mercy and good fruits. Wisdom and understanding is manifest in these works. A meekness of wisdom is the character of those who work these works of God.

CHAPTER 13

THE FRUIT OF COMPASSION

I am breaking you down to love the least. I am giving you the honor of knowing Him who is lowly and meek and found among them. For I have not called you to the profession of "ministry," but to the hidden service of the undefiled.

I've called you to be an oil soaked vessel oozing with My burden and compassion for broken humanity. I've called you to the highways and the hedges of lost mankind. I've called you to see them through My mind. I've called you to point the way for others who have been left behind.

So many of My people have forgotten the ones I love. They have forsaken the path that leads to My heart. They have forgotten their Apostle and High Priest of their profession Who bore the infirmities of every man and was sent to be the Captain of all their salvation. I renew you, son with My salvation. I beautify you with the meekness of the Son.

Look at My people. See My body. Where are the laborers for My harvest? Shame is the inheritance of those who sleep in harvest. They make their beds in the spoils of their own success. They revel in the path of carnal enjoyment and rejoice in the pleasures of this earthly life. The seed of the compassion of the Son is choked within under layers of the leaven of hypocrisy.

I seek for My priests to stand in the gap for those who cannot stand for themselves. I seek for My captains to lead the way in the mission of this rescue. Will you be one?

"How?" you ask. First, begin by hearing and bearing these words in your heart for they are the instruction of the wise. The wise son makes a glad Father. A wise son works His Father's harvest.

Secondly, pray. Pray for My seed of compassion to grow in My people. Pray that they would be rooted and grounded in My love for others.

Thirdly, work. Work among My forgotten ones when you can. I will send you on assignments.

Finally, write and speak for this My love. Be a pen inked with My ointment. Be a mouthpiece with lips that drip with words from the travail of My heart. Let your bowels be moved by My mercies.

This shall be your emergence from the muck and mire of the profession of "ministry" and into the compassions of the Son's great heart. This is the image I now impart. Do not let it depart.

It will help you immeasurably to always pray for those I send you to. Pray for those you speak to. Incorporate prayer with all your speaking. Incorporate prayer with all your goings and comings. Pray before and after. Water the soil of all your service with prayer, and My seed of compassion shall grow. The water is the prayers for My people.

I will help you in supplying the ability that produces results in both you and those I send you to. The results will be the fruit of My compassion.

Behold now, the fertility of this your virgin womb! I give you My compassion. These are My seeds of implantation and growth. For you, implantation comes before implementation. You must forget your old ways for I open the veil of new days (to open the veil of new days means to behold the glory of the Lord with an unveiled face and be transformed into His image, from glory to glory). The curtain is drawn back and the light of a new dawning now appears as the Daystar in your heart now shines. As the breaking of the morning and as the dew on the grass, revelation now dawns and settles upon you with freshness.

The fruit of this compassion shall be souls. The fruit of this compassion shall be revelation and power. The fruit of this compassion shall be a skillful anointing of a mercy mixed with might.

And yes, I can give you My revelation and power without My compassion, but that is not My best. Have you not asked Me for My best? My perfect birthing is for My gifts of revelation and power and utterance to be the fruit of My compassion in you. The fruit of My Spirit is to be the foundation of the gifts of My Spirit. Does not My Word say to follow and pursue the fruit of love while at the same time desiring spiritual gifts?

Many men have aborted their ministries because of an imperfect birthing of My power without My love and compassion. For many, the implementation of their gifts and ministries came without proper implantation and growth of the seeds of My love and compassion. Much damage has been done because of the immaturity in flowing in the love and compassion of the Son. I would not have you be one. I would have you be damage proof (no miscarriages or abortions).

The needs of My forgotten people have been neglected. My body has failed to carry out their daily ministration. My priests have failed to pray and stand in the gap. My captains have not heralded the cause. And so there's been a pause…

Impure religion has bound so many and the profession of "ministry" has brought a pause to the ministry of My compassion. Compassion moves; it does not pause. There's been a pause in My compassion, but it must move again so that the least will not be last, so that the least will not be lost, so that there may be joy in My house again.

Personal comments: There is a definite order in the last three documents. It is one continuous message much like all of these documents. It is amazing to me how the Spirit of God can speak to you over a period of many weeks and months and build on each revelation and truth. The key to receiving this kind of revelation is to spend much time praying in other tongues. I have read and meditated on the message in these last three documents because it contains the real heart of the Lord.

CHAPTER 14

ABASEMENT, ABIDING, ABOUNDING

(Phil 4:10-19) (1 Cor 4:11) (Lk 18:14) (John 15:1-8)

In a land of plenty where there is bread and wine in sufficiency, **abasement** does not come easily. In a land of materialism where money is in sufficiency, abasement is not learned easily. In a land where there is little persecution and suffering for the gospel's sake, there is almost no meekness of soul found among My people.

Paul not only received revelation of the redemption from all the curse of the law which includes poverty, but for the gospel's sake he also learned to suffer hunger and thirst and a lack of decent living conditions. In whatever state he was in, he learned to be content.

Contentment is a state of meekness of soul. Contentment keeps you free from working where I am not working and moving where I am not moving. Contentment in Me will keep you from fighting conditions that are uncomfortable to the flesh. Anger, impatience, and frustration cease in a state of contentment. Contend for contentment which comes through meekness of soul.

As long as My people are bound by covetousness they will never **abound** in possessing the true riches of My glory. Covetousness is a state of wanting something more than Me and My true riches.

Perfect contentment in Me through meekness of soul is required to hear My voice and learn My ways. The humbling or abasement of the soul is when you lay down your own will and agenda on the altar of My life. Fasting in the Old Covenant was a tool they often used to humble their souls. In the New Covenant, this tool will accomplish the same results.

Fasting does not change Me; it changes you. The only difference between the two covenants when it comes to fasting is that in the New Covenant you have a new spiritual nature to help you overcome.

As an example, unbelief is a part of man's soul. Unbelief is a stronghold in man's fleshly nature that can only be dealt a death blow through prayer and fasting. Fasting is one of the ways to acquire meekness of soul where you are no longer operating the works of God out of your own strength. Fasting helps you acquire the position of intimate silence. This is a place of breaking down the stubbornness and rebellion of your own will until you reach the position of intimate silence where My peace rules your soul.

This quietness of soul is your true strength. It is a place where your own strength subsides and you take on My strength. This is the true meaning of, "in weakness you are made strong." In quietness of soul is where you will hear My counsel.

While fasting is a tool used to accomplish an abasing of your soul, praying in other tongues is a tool for the edification of your spirit. You have used these well, and your diligence in them is to be commended. However, I would have you step up your diligence in the exercise of the meditation of My Word. To move from the position of abasement to that of **abiding** more meditation is required. You have known this in your spirit.

Meekness of soul is acquired and maintained through a continued process of abasement. My Word can only be received and engrafted into your soul through meekness. My Word cannot be engrafted into a soul that has not been abased. The process of abasement should follow the conversion of a soul, but so often it does not because the will has not changed ownership. My will is not only for My people to be My children but to also be bond-servants to the Son.

My words cannot abide in a soul that has not been abased. My words cannot abide in one who is still seeking to do his own will. One who has not laid down his own will for Mine is not a true disciple. My kingdom and rule cannot manifest in such a one. This is why so many do not hear My voice. That is also why their judgment is not just. They do not have My mind because they do not genuinely seek My will. When My words abide in you, what you will shall also be My will. My desire shall be your desire. We shall be one. There will be no division between us.

The problem with many of My children is that they want My will in a carnal manner (this is why the new wine is lacking). Just as My own disciples imagined an earthly Messiah setting up an earthly throne, so it is today concerning the mind of My people. Even when My will is known, the methods to accomplish that will are so often perverse and wrong. This is another reason why I cannot speak more of My counsel to more of My people. Their minds have not been developed to think like Me. Their methods are based on human logic and human wisdom. My ways are so often different from their ways, and My thoughts higher than their thoughts.

I have given you My Word in order for your mind to conform to My will. Unless this conforming takes place, My people will remain in an infant state and My body will continue to lack discernment. My words can only abide in a mind that is conformed to My will. This is what My Word means by the "saving of the soul." Obedience is required to prove this.

When your mind has been developed to think like Me then I will give you more instructions for obedience. Obedience will sometimes come with suffering. As it was with the Son, so it is with all who desire to walk in My perfect will. Suffering is a part of obedience to My will. This is especially true at increased levels of glory. Another way to say it is obedience is learned through suffering, and suffering for My will births My glory. This is also why fasting is important. It breaks down the outer man and humbles the soul to condition it for obedience in suffering.

The religions of the world fast, you say, but without My life and nature in them and without My Word, their fasting only strengthens the power of their own will to fulfill their own thoughts and purposes. Religion causes sin to abound. My new nature causes grace to abound. When a person chooses My Son he is given a new nature and My grace immediately begins to work in him to will and to do of My good pleasure.

The seed of My life and nature is in you. Through the meditation of My Word that seed takes root and grows to where it becomes that tree planted by the rivers of water. The phrase, "If you abide in Me," is the maturity of the seed of My life to branch level. The phrase, "If My words abide in you," is the maturity of that branch to fruit level.

Those who sacrifice My life and nature on the altar of their own will are as branches that bear *no fruit*. Those who sacrifice a part of their will on the altar of My life and nature are as branches that bear *some fruit*. Those who sacrifice more and more of their own will on the altar of My life and nature are as branches who bear more and *more fruit*. Those who have placed all their will on the altar of My life and nature and have proven it by their obedience are as branches that bear *much fruit*.

I give you another instruction from My grace. I give you another instruction for the discipline of your soul and for the mortification of your flesh. A willingness and an obedience to this instruction will further strengthen your spirit. You have been found diligent in all matters of discipline, and the Father is pleased with your obedience.

The instruction that I now bring from the Father is to extend this fast of three days to six days. Obedience to this instruction will bring another measure of the mind of Christ to you. The Father will reward you openly.

As you first heard this instruction, you were unwilling. You wanted to dismiss it as only your own thoughts. There are two reasons why many of My people do not hear My instructions. One is because they do not take time to wait on Me. The second reason is that they only hear what they want to hear. They only hear what appeals to their unharnessed soul and to the will of their own emotions. This is what is meant by the phrase, "sacrificing My life and nature on the altar of your own will." The only place for a strong will is on the altar of the life and nature of the Son.

Your willingness to the exercise of obedience in the more difficult and illogical instructions will accelerate the development of your mind being conformed to the mind of Christ, and will also expand the capacity of the ability of your heart to trust Me. You will develop in the confidence that you are hearing Me. My words will abide in you and you will bear much fruit.

Because of your hunger and your diligence to obey all My instructions and to fulfill all of My will, much wisdom has been given to you in a very short time. I am pleased with the sacrifice of your own will on the altar of My life and nature. Sacrifice without obedience is the pride of religion and an affront to the glorious life and liberty that is in the Son. Obedience with sacrifice is pure religion and well pleasing to the Father. He who loves Me obeys Me and keeps My commandments. This is the true law of liberty and the gospel of My grace.

My love for you does not change no matter what you do, no matter if you obey or disobey. But the communion of the Father and the Son through Me will not be enjoyed by those who do not hear and keep My commandments. You are enjoying My communion because you have been found willing and obedient to all My instructions. I have shared much with you because of the time you've sown in prayer and waiting on Me, and also because of your diligence to obedience. At the end of these next three days I will call you friend.

You are on a journey to transformation and a glory where you will never have to guess, wonder, or assume whether you are hearing My voice. Your willingness and obedience to today's instructions, though it appears small, places you up higher to another rung of the ladder of My transformation and glory. I have granted you My companionship and communion through the fear of the Lord I have found in your heart. Again, this is the beginning of the growth of My wisdom in you.

At the end of these next three days your joy shall be made full and the Father and the Son will manifest themselves to you in friendship, and you shall understand the meaning of John 15:11 and John 14:23. Expect My presence and the wine of My love. Welcome to My dwelling place and the table of My dining.

I strengthen you now for the next three days. Enjoy My grace. Remain in Me.

CHAPTER 15

SONS OF THE FLESH

Sons of the flesh are those that depend on the strength of their own arm to produce the results and the fruit that only God can produce. Most training schools, and Bible colleges or institutes today are producing sons of the flesh who cannot inherit the promise of power. This is a kind of slavery as there was in Egypt long ago that keeps men bound to human philosophies and to human techniques that are void of My instruction and My counsel.

There is a kind of slavery in My body and in these schools of ministry. There is a slavery to men's doctrines and men's traditions which I desire to bring My people out of. It is a slavery of rigor and hard bondage, of toiling at the mill, and of the sweat of face. This is part of the curse of the fall that came on Adam which I have delivered My children from.

I desire not ministry to become rigorous and tend to hard bondage. I desire not ministry to be made from the sweat of your face. But I desire it all to be done by My Spirit and by My grace, and with My yoke which is not hard or burdensome but easy and light. My yoke is simple obedience to My counsel and to My voice. In My yoke is freedom and not slavery. True freedom is to be one with Me.

What training school did the Son enroll in? And who taught Him and who equipped Him to work the works of God?

The Son found Himself in scripture. The image of who He was revealed to be by the prophets in the Old Testament was planted in His spirit and soul through revelation. The testimony of His earthly parents bore witness to this also. He subjected Himself to His earthly parents while being taught by His Heavenly Father.

CHAPTER 16

CLASSROOMS OF THE SPIRIT

There are many classrooms of My Spirit with many courses. Each classroom has its own course. "Learning To Hear My Voice" is one of the greatest courses. Most of My children live and die and never go into this classroom. They never learn to hear My voice, and so they never develop a living faith. They never learn to commune with Me and they never work the works of God. This is a grievous thing to My Spirit who has been sent for this very purpose.

Two other of the major foundational courses to the development of My ministers which are taught in the classrooms of My Spirit are "The Management of Home Affairs" and "The Management of The Tongue."

"The Management of Home Affairs" is foundational for obvious reasons. How shall a man rule the house of God if he cannot rule his own house? "The Management of The Tongue" is also foundational for the simple reason of the entrusting of My Word. How can I entrust My Word to someone who cannot keep his own word? Your word is connected to your spirit. If a man cannot govern his spirit, he becomes like a city broken down and without walls. He is an open target for the enemy. But a man who has learned to bridle his tongue is a perfect or a mature man. It is not My will for immaturity to be a leader of My people.

The man with an unruly house and an unruly tongue disqualifies himself from hearing any further counsel except to get his house in order and tame his tongue. Why should I give My counsel to such a one? Would you give your seven year old instructions fit for a mature son? I would violate My justice and cease to be a responsible Father if I did so. To give one such counsel would be an act of cruelty as opposed to mercy.

The discipline of the tongue is the greatest; hear Me, it is the greatest of all the disciplines. Pay more attention to the discipline of silence. I would not just have you refrain from speaking wrong words or evil words. I would not just have you refrain from speaking negative words or words of strife or criticism. But I would also have you refrain your tongue from speaking some of My counsel and My wisdom and revelation, for there is a time and a season to speak. This is a very important word for you as you grow in hearing more of My counsel.

There is not only a set time to speak, but also a set place and people to speak it to. I would not have you speak My counsel to anyone who would not receive it. I would not have My counsel fall on deaf ears. I will give you wisdom when and who to speak to. And I will teach you how to speak My counsel so that it is heard every time. I will also show you when not to speak and who would not receive My counsel.

Learn the discipline of silence for I would have you be exercised much more in this discipline than you presently are. You have learned many valuable lessons in this, but you must increase this discipline among men. Just as you are learning to listen more than you speak in My presence so I would have you do so in the presence of men.

Is this not My wisdom? Is this not where My wisdom begins? Does not My Word say that a man is counted wise when he maintains silence?

Personal comments: When I received this word I kept having the impression of a hallway with different classrooms. On each door of

each classroom was a sign of the course taught in that classroom. So it is in the Spirit.

CHAPTER 17

MEEKNESS AND MIRACLES

ADDRESSING CHARACTER AND CALLING

You are climbing on Jacob's ladder where angels ascend and descend. For the wisdom that is from above is first pure, then peaceable, easy to be entreated, and full of mercy and good fruits. And so you are climbing into the wisdom and works of the Father. My son, My son, My son, keep on climbing.

And I will move you on into power. I will move you on into healings and miracles. With you I am completing this season of the instructions of discipline. You have been willing and you have been obedient. Your diligence has pleased Me, and as I complete one phase of this training and this discipline, I move you on to the study of the realm of power and the realm of miracles. You shall add this to the study of the holiness of My Son and the meekness of His soul. There shall be a simultaneous study of both of these attributes of the Son for He was a man of great meekness and a man of great miracles. The instructions of My discipline is for the development of meekness before the power.

I will add miracles to your meekness. As you meditate on the miracles of the Son, I will lift you up another rung, another rung, and another rung on that ladder. And you will climb to that place where angels will ascend and descend upon you. I establish you in the instructions of My discipline so that you may move on to the transformation of My love. This is the first work and the foundation. But I also will move you on into power.

You are at a place now of the 40 days where the Son was led into the wilderness and He fasted and prayed and resisted Satan. Then it is written that He came out in the power of the Spirit. Know also that it shall be the same with you. And as you continue on in the instructions of discipline, I will move you on into an understanding, and then into a manifestation of My power heretofore you have not known. In this the Son's righteousness shall be fulfilled in you for in the past many have walked in a power without meekness, but you will possess both.

Personal comments: Once again, even though this is a personal word there is much in it for ministers. As you can see once more, meekness was a common theme throughout this time of seeking the Lord.

Here are some other scriptures the Holy Spirit quickened to me concerning meekness:

"He who is slow to anger is better than the mighty, and he who rules his spirit than he who takes a city." (Pr 16:32)

"Whoever has no rule over his own spirit is like a spirit broken down, without walls." (Pr 25:28)

"Now the man Moses was very meek, more than all men who were on the face of the earth." (Num 12:3)

"Take My yoke upon you and learn from Me, for I am meek and lowly in heart (Literally means, "low to the ground." Metaphorically, the word signifies low estate, lowly in position and power), and you will find rest for your souls." (Mat 11:29)

"Now I, Paul, myself am pleading with you by the meekness and gentleness of Christ..." (2 Cor 10:1)

Isn't it interesting that three of the greatest men in the Bible, Moses, Jesus, and Paul possessed a spirit of meekness? Could this also be the reason they had such an ear for the word of the Lord? And worked so many miracles? If you don't have an ear you don't have a mouth.

"The Lord has given me the tongue of the learned, that I should know how to speak a word in season to him who is weary. He awakens Me morning by morning, He awakens My ear to hear as the learned." (Isa 50:4)

Do you desire to walk in the blessing of an open ear? The key is cultivating the meekness of the Lamb.

"The Lord God has opened My ear; and I was not rebellious, nor did I turn away. I gave My back to those who struck Me, and My cheeks to those who plucked out the beard; I did not hide My face from shame and spitting." (Isa 50:5-6)

CHAPTER 18

THE CAMPS OF MAN AND THE COURTS OF GOD

"Neither on this mountain nor in Jerusalem shall men worship the Father" (John 4:21). These are the camps of man. Camps of man are places confined to the limitations of the flesh. But to worship in spirit and in truth (v 23) shall place you into the courts of your God.

And it is true worship in the courts of your God that will enlarge you in the camps of man. Behold how the camp of man enlarged for the Son wherever He went! In John 4, one woman, one conversation, and then enlargement! Many others came to hear Him and believed (John 4:28-30, 39). Behold what the ministry of the Spirit produced! This was the pattern in the life and ministry of the Son and in the lives of those He trained.

The Son was a worshiper. He could always be found in the high courts of His Father. The camp of man was being continually enlarged in His life and ministry. People came from round about to hear the Master Teacher. People came from round about to be healed by the Great Physician. People came from round about seeking Him (Lk 4:42) (Mk 1:35-37).

The Son only walked where He had inheritance. It was the ministry of the Spirit through the Son that enlarged His steps and caused Him to possess His inheritance. Your inheritance is possessed the same way.

The expansion of the ministry of the Spirit in the camp of man always happens in proportion to the hearing and obeying of His counsel in the courts of God. What you have today is a perversion of the true works of God. Expansion in the camp of man through the sons of flesh happens much today through natural means by marketing and promotional techniques. This would be no different than a business which brings in profit through marketing and promoting their product.

The only place for marketing and promotion in My kingdom is through the fruit of obeying the Spirit's counsel. Remember, you do not create ministry in order to produce fruit. You listen and obey the Spirit and then the fruit of your obedience creates ministry. There is a vast difference between the two.

The woman at the well was the fruit of the Son's obedience to the Father. The fruit created more ministry (John 4:28-30, 39). Once again, this was the pattern established not only from the Son and the early apostles, but even from the days of the Old Covenant through those whom I anointed.

Truly My house has become a house of merchandise instead of a house of prayer. And this is My zeal that I've put in you. My zeal for your call is to elevate the courts of God above the ways of man. My zeal for your call is for you to walk in the demonstration of this word. Many will not hear you, but many will. Many more will hear you as this word is demonstrated.

The wisdom of God is manifest in the weakness of the flesh. The power of God is manifest in the weakness of the flesh.

ENLARGEMENT

As a young calf loosed from its stall
The Lord has enlarged my place
No more confinement to the way of man

No more being confined by the flesh

My steps have been enlarged
The Lord has made the way
By the light of His counsel
He brightens my every day

I seek not the honor of man
But I seek only the honor of God
I seek not enlargement in the camp of man
But I seek only enlargement in the courts of My God

CHAPTER 19

FOUND IN HIM WHO MOVES

Taste this anointing now that settles upon you. It is the ministry of the Holy Spirit. You shall know Him now in a way you have not known Him before. You shall understand Him now in a way you have not understood Him before. Even last night marks a beginning for you in moving with the flow of My Spirit. Taste it now. See that it is easy. See that it is light. See that it is fluid and free flowing like water from your heart.

I will take you into different streams of My flow. You will understand the Holy Spirit when He is ready to heal the sick and manifest His miracle power. You shall know Him in that stream. You shall also know Him in that stream of revelation and greater depths of prophecy where the word of the Lord is coming forth and being imparted into the hearts of the people.

You shall know Him in joy and laughter. You shall also know Him in the severity of My judgments and the word of repentance. You shall know him in My holiness and in My power.

You shall be like Nicodemus of old who did not know where the wind came from nor where it goes. He only knew its presence. You shall know when the Holy Spirit comes. I school you in these things now. You shall know His touch. You shall know His breath. You shall know the wind of His flow and His power. And you shall flow and be found again in Him who moves. Have I not spoken it to you? Have I not said it to you several times that I do a work in you that you might be found in Him who moves.

Personal comments: I found this expression, "found in Him who moves" to be very interesting and profound. In Him we are to live and move and have our being. Again, a private word, but something here for everyone to glean from. It is one thing to look for the move of God, but quite another thing to have the move in you.

But know that I am teaching you to sense that breath, to sense that hearing of the wind, and to wade out into those waters by faith. And that door will open to you wider and wider as you learn to yield, and you will understand more of the meaning of "rivers of living water". For those rivers will take you whichever way they turn. There will be a diversity of anointings that you shall become more familiar with.

It will be as a door that opens into the light. It will be as a person coming in from a dark or dim-lit corridor into the opening of a door of glorious light. And you shall open that door and peek in and your spiritual eyes shall see this and see that, and you shall see My Spirit moving on this one and that one and I will give you revelation concerning them. And suddenly in a flash you shall know things about their lives, about their past, about their present, and even about their future. I will school you and train you to flow in this stream of My Spirit.

So take comfort in knowing that it will not be difficult. Moving with Me is not a difficult thing. Just as you would walk down the street with a partner or a friend; just as you were to follow a leader down a path. You will see Me and you will do what you see Me do. You will say what you hear Me say. It will not be difficult. It will not be rigid. So take comfort in knowing that My flow is easy. This is My grace and it shall become second nature to you. Behold, I am training you privately even now.

Yes, you shall become familiar with My coming ins and My going outs. You will become familiar with My manifestations. You will know when I have come, and you will know what I have come for as you wait on Me. You will know. And you will also know when I have lifted, and when I have moved out or when I have moved on to something else. The operations will change and you will know it.

And so the way of My Spirit shall not be spoiled by performance in the flesh. The way of My Spirit shall not be spoiled by going beyond the anointing. For when My anointing lifts or when My anointing stops, you shall stop. When My anointing changes operations, you too shall change.

Personal comments: Oh how we need to heed this especially as ministers!

I am speaking into your ear, son. I am teaching you these things. For you shall not only have an ear for My Spirit, but you shall have an eye for what He is doing. And you will have an eye into things, situations, and lives. You will have a big eye. You will have a clear eye. I give you the eye of an eagle. You will see deep and wide. I will take you on into these things. I will take you on into a deeper revealing and deeper unveiling and unfolding. I will train your eye to see near and far.

This is a living word that produces in you a living faith. Do not doubt this word, but let it produce in you a lasting image of the flow of Him who moves.

ABOUT THE AUTHOR

Bert M. Farias, together with his wife, Carolyn, graduates of Rhema Bible Training Center, founded Holy Fire Ministries in 1997 after serving for nine years as missionaries in West Africa, establishing nation-changing interdenominational Bible training centers with an organization called Living Word Missions.

From 1999 to 2003, Bert served as the internship coordinator on the senior leadership team of the Brownsville Revival School of Ministry and Fire School of Ministry in Pensacola, Florida, a school birthed from a massive, heaven-sent revival that brought approximately four million visitors from around the world, with an estimated 150,000 first-time conversions. There, Rev. Farias and his wife taught and mentored young men and women in the call of God and trained them for the work of the ministry.

Bert is a messenger of the Lord carrying a spirit of revival to the Church and the nations. An anointing of fire marks his ministry with frequent demonstrations of the Spirit and the power of God. With a divine commission to also write, Bert has authored several books with an emphasis on helping to restore the true spirit of Christianity in the Church today and preparing the saints for the glory of God, the harvest, and the imminent return of the Lord.

Before being dedicated solely to the full-time preaching and teaching ministry, Bert experienced a unique and powerful baptism of fire. His consuming passion is for human beings to come into a real and vibrant relationship with the Lord Jesus Christ through the power of the Holy Spirit and to become passionate workers in His kingdom, thus preparing them for the second coming of Christ, being among the wise virgins and a part of the first-fruits harvest who will gain an abundant entrance into glory and receive a sure reward.

Bert currently resides in Windham, New Hampshire, with his beautiful wife, Carolyn. They are proud parents of one precious son of promise.

OTHER BOOKS BY BERT M. FARIAS

SOULISH LEADERSHIP

This book is for everyone…
- Who longs for purity of heart.
- Who desires to be set aright in the core of his being.
- Who dreads God's disapproval more than man's.
- Whose greatest phobia is the fear of a wasted life and burned-up works.

The works that endure the testing of God's holy fire will one day be rewarded. Others will suffer loss (1 Cor 3:12-15). Will your works stand the fire or will they go up in smoke?

In that day the motive of every heart will be made clear. Leaders will be judged by a higher standard. Only one question will matter then, and it's the same question that matters now: Are you building your kingdom or the kingdom of God?

THE REAL SPIRIT OF REVIVAL

In this book, Bert challenges the status quo of Christianity today and redefines its true spirit which is one of revival and of living the Spirit filled life. With one eye on the coming glory of the Lord and His soon return, and another eye on the harvest of souls yet to be reached, *The Real Spirit Of Revival* takes the reader into a preparation to becoming a true lover of Jesus and a passionate worker in His kingdom. These vital truths that dot each new chapter of this book are sure to awaken you as one from a deep sleep, and light a fire in your soul.

If you are tired of a mundane relationship with God and desire to burn with His holy fire this book is a must read.

THE REAL GOSPEL

With piercing prophetic insight this book exposes the fallacies and shortcuts in the modern gospel and calls us back to Jesus and the cross. Its message reveals why so many Christians and churches today lack power, endurance, and character. Written in the spirit, style, and plainness of speech of the old timers, it breathes into today's shallow gospel the life of the spirit of holiness, giving us fresh eyes on old truths.

This is a critical book for the hour – a real wake up call to all. Backed by an abundance of scripture *The Real Gospel* is as truthful as it is radical.

THE REAL SALVATION

Can you imagine feeling secure in a salvation you don't even possess? Such is the state of mass humanity today. We have libraries full of sermons yet still so much confusion and deception about what the real salvation is. With poignancy and pinpoint clarity this short and sweet book cuts through the fat of satanic philosophy, exposes the deception of the broad way of religion, and shines the light on the narrow path to eternal life.

Most books are 200 pages with 30 pages worthwhile, and 170 of fluff. *The Real Salvation* is less than 60 pages, but every word counts. Make it count for you and your unsaved friends and loved ones!

PURITY OF HEART

The primary basis of all judgment concerning the deeds done in our bodies is our motives. Our values determine our motives, and our motives are the real reason behind our thoughts, words, and deeds. Only God can see the true motives of every man's heart.

Almost all human beings have something to hide. Nearly everyone twists words, events, and situations to their own advantage, to place themselves in the best possible light. Men often have ulterior motives and hidden agendas. This is sin and a form of hiding.

Adam and Eve first hid from the presence of the Lord in the garden after they had fallen. But there will be no hiding from the presence of the Lord on that solemn Day of Judgment.

Purity of Heart will prepare you for that day and spare you loss at the judgment seat of Christ so that you may receive your full reward. What is done in pure love, by the leading of the Spirit, and for the glory and honor of God shall reap the fullest rewards.

PRAYER: LANGUAGE OF THE SPIRIT

Prayer: The Language Of The Spirit is a short and poignant book that helps lay a foundation from the Word for knowing and walking with God. Each chapter directs the earnest believer into possessing a life of communion with God and praying without ceasing.

Prayer is walking with God. It is habitual fellowship with God. You can walk so close to God that you feel like you're in heaven. The key that will move you toward this richness of communion with Him is to not only know the Word but to cultivate a receptivity and sensitivity to His Spirit and presence.

You can experience this kind of life in God if you will pursue Him. It all begins with receiving the baptism of the Holy Spirit and praying extensively in other tongues. This is the language of the Spirit.

PASSING ON THE MOVE OF GOD
TO THE NEXT GENERATION

This book, *Passing on the Move of God to the Next Generation*, is like a template for the New Testament Church. Its words act as a plumb line that will help restore the uncompromised Word and the fullness of the Spirit back to our pulpits and churches.

When we compare the Word that the early apostles preached and that of our more recent Pentecostal forefathers, we find a depth and richness rarely evidenced today. Additionally, there was also an understanding and accuracy in spiritual operations that are clearly missing from normal Pentecostal and Charismatic experience in this generation.

But there is a hunger stirring at our spiritual tables, and a thirst screaming out from the deep wells that have been dug from past fathers of the faith. Can you hear the winds of God blowing and the sound of the abundance of rain?

Bert Farias blows the trumpet loud and clear, summoning the Church and its preachers to return to the authenticity of the Scriptures and their Pentecostal roots of Spirit and fire (Acts 2). If we heed this call, it can turn the tide of ignorance, apathy, and compromise and flood our churches again with the real move of the Holy Spirit.

MY SON, MY SON

This book is one of the most unique books on father-son relationships you will ever find. Co-written by father and son, it has a personal touch and intimate tone that will leave you teary-eyed one moment and then rejoicing the next. Within its pages you will find a spiritual quality of training and a godly example of shepherding children that will both enrich and empower parents. It also offers hope for those parents who have fallen short or started late in their child training.

Fathers, your son (or daughter) is typically in your home for an average of 18-20 years before he ventures out independently to navigate his own little boat in this world's turbulent waters. Until then, with God's help, you, more than anyone else, have the greatest opportunity to shape him and mold him into the man he will eventually become. You've got one shot at being a father. Make it count.

MINISTRY INFORMATION

To become a monthly partner with Holy Fire Ministries, schedule a speaking engagement with Bert, or to receive the ministry's free newsletter please contact:

Holy Fire Ministries
P. O. Box 4527
Windham, NH 03087

Web: www.holy-fire.org

Email: adm@holy-fire.org

Made in the USA
San Bernardino, CA
14 March 2017